THE SUPREME DIPLOMAT
HANUMAN'S
ART OF WAR & PEACE

LAL BHATIA

INDIA • SINGAPORE • MALAYSIA

ISBN 979-8-89929-358-0

"To my daughters,
Karishma and **Nisha**—

The only strategists I know who can outwit me with a single glance, negotiate like seasoned diplomats, and run circles around logic with charm and sarcasm.

You are my greatest victories, my daily lessons in leadership, and living proof that brilliance comes with a side of mischief."

TABLE OF CONTENTS

ABOUT THE AUTHOR: DR. LAL BHATIA

Dr. Lal Bhatia is a visionary trailblazer redefining success through intellect, innovation, and action. With over 35 years of transformative impact, he has emerged as a thought leader, advisor to royalty, author, poet, investor, and philosopher who seamlessly bridges the worlds of business, sustainability, and the arts.

Armed with advanced degrees, including a Master's in Business Administration, a Doctorate in Business Administration, and an honorary doctorate in Business Strategy and Tactical Acquisitions, Dr. Bhatia has dedicated his life to challenging norms and driving strategic growth across industries and borders. As the architect behind David & Goliath Films, Farms, and Carbon, he leads ventures that redefine excellence, sustainability, and storytelling.

Under his leadership, David & Goliath Films has earned 36 awards and over 50 accolades globally in just three years. From triumphs at the Cannes World Film Festival to the Dada Saheb Phalke Film Festival and the Global Music Awards, his work has captivated hearts and minds across continents, making him one of the most recognized names in transformative cinema. As the Executive Producer of the *Twisted Truths Podcast*, Dr. Bhatia delivers actionable insights and life strategies, amplifying his impact in shaping future-forward narratives.

In the realm of sustainability, Dr. Bhatia's innovative ventures with David & Goliath Farms have raised €5 million through groundbreaking carbon credit forward contracts. This initiative exemplifies the seamless integration of sustainability and profitability, setting new benchmarks for eco-services and agriculture aligned with the UAE's vision for a green economy.

A media magnet and celebrated leader, Dr. Bhatia has graced the covers of *Khaleej Times*, *Entrepreneur Magazine*, and *Arabian Business* and has been featured on platforms like Bloomberg, CNBC News, and BBC World News. Whether commanding attention at the 1 Billion Followers Summit or a fireside chat at the Arabian Business Forum, his insights on leadership, innovation, and social impact leave indelible marks on global audiences.

Recognized as the "Visionary of the Year 2022" by *Entrepreneur Magazine* and celebrated for entrepreneurial excellence by St. Xavier's College and the *Times of India*, Dr. Bhatia embodies the spirit of bold innovation and service. His work sparks conversations that matter, inspiring businesses, governments, and individuals to create a greener, more innovative, and equitable world.

From Dubai to the world stage, Dr. Lal Bhatia is not just a leader but a movement—one dedicated to shaping a future where sustainability meets profitability, art sparks dialogue, and leadership redefines its purpose.

ACKNOWLEDGEMENTS

They say heroes are timeless, and none prove this better than Hanuman—the original multitasker, diplomat, and problem-solver extraordinaire. This book owes its existence to the monkey god who could teach modern leaders a thing or two about managing crises, building alliances, and, let's not forget, carrying mountains like a pro.

To the ancient poets who immortalized Hanuman's exploits—thank you for writing epics that keep us wondering if we're dreaming big enough. To the scholars, thinkers, and armchair philosophers who dissected his wisdom and argued over his lessons, your debates fuelled my curiosity and, frankly, kept me entertained.

To my tireless support system—you didn't just encourage me to write; you tolerated my endless musings about a mythical hero's leadership style. You're the real MVPs, even if you now know more about Hanuman than you ever planned to.

And, of course, to Hanuman himself—this one's for you. You showed us that faith and intelligence can move mountains (literally), and that being underestimated is the best weapon in any strategist's arsenal. If only modern leaders had your humility, humor, and knack for quick thinking, we'd be in a far better place.

Lastly, to you, dear reader, welcome to the club. By picking up this book, you've officially joined the "Hanuman Fan Society." Let's hope his lessons inspire you to lead boldly, think differently, and maybe, just maybe, carry a mountain or two of your own.

Here's to Hanuman—part god, part monkey, and full-time legend.

– Dr. Lal Bhatia

INTRODUCTION

SETTING THE STAGE

Key Takeaways

- *Balance of Power and Wisdom*: Hanuman's ability to combine physical strength with strategic thinking. Like Tim Cook at Apple - Known for his calm, diplomatic approach in contrast to Jobs' forceful style, Cook has successfully navigated Apple through challenges like privacy battles and trade wars using strategic thinking rather than aggressive confrontation. Under his leadership, Apple's value has grown through careful diplomacy and strategic decisions.

- *Intelligence Gathering & Analysis*: Hanuman's reconnaissance of Lanka before the war. Like Microsoft's Satya Nadella's cloud-first strategy came after careful market analysis. Before making major moves in cloud computing, he studied market trends, competitor strengths, and customer needs, transforming Microsoft from a PC-software company to a cloud computing leader.

- *Strategic Alliance Building*: Hanuman bridging Rama and Sugriva's alliance. Like the Netflix-Marvel partnership (2013-2018) orchestrated by Reed Hastings. This strategic alliance helped Netflix establish itself in original content production while giving Marvel a new platform, demonstrating how partnerships can create mutual benefit.

- *Emotional Intelligence in Leadership*: Hanuman's ability to understand and navigate human emotions. Like Jacinda Ardern's leadership during the Christchurch tragedy. Her combination of empathy and decisive action demonstrated how modern leaders can balance emotional intelligence with strong decision-making.

- *Timing and Tactical Patience*: Hanuman knowing when to use force and when to use diplomacy. Like AMD's Lisa Su's patient strategy to compete with Intel. Instead of directly challenging Intel's dominance, she focused on specific market segments and gradually built AMD's strength, leading to significant market share gains through careful timing and strategic patience.

In the vast tapestry of Indian mythology, there is perhaps no figure more captivating than Hanuman, the mighty monkey god. His stories are woven into the very fabric of India's spiritual and cultural consciousness—tales that speak of his unwavering devotion to Lord Rama, his superhuman strength, and his heroic feats that often defy the limits of imagination. Across ages and generations, Hanuman has been celebrated as a symbol of courage, loyalty, and humility. But behind the tales of physical might and divine loyalty lies a lesser-known side to this legendary figure—a side that reveals him as a master diplomat, a shrewd strategist, and a tactician whose wisdom shaped the course of history.

The story of Hanuman is not simply the story of battles fought and won, nor is it merely a testament to devotion in its purest form. It is a narrative of intellect meeting intuition, of strategy interwoven with compassion. It is the story of a mind that could discern the most complex human motives, negotiate peace amidst chaos, and see beyond the immediate to the long-term consequences of each decision. It is this rarely explored side of Hanuman that forms the heart of this book—his ability to wield words as effectively as he could wield a mace, to find pathways where others saw walls, and to turn adversaries into allies with nothing but the strength of his character and the sharpness of his intellect.

Our journey begins in the shadowed forests of Kishkindha, where Hanuman first steps into the role of a diplomat, bringing together the exiled prince Rama and the beleaguered monkey king Sugriva. This seemingly simple act of alliance-building becomes a turning point, demonstrating how Hanuman's wisdom could lay the groundwork for a larger plan that would eventually shake the very foundations of the demon-king Ravana's reign. It is in these moments of negotiation and persuasion that we see a glimpse of Hanuman's strategic mind—a mind capable of assessing a situation with clarity, identifying opportunities amidst turmoil, and guiding his allies with a balance of humility and confidence.

As Hanuman ventures beyond the shores of India to the island kingdom of Lanka, his journey transforms into one of reconnaissance and intelligence gathering. He does not merely leap across oceans; he navigates the currents of power, studying Ravana's fortress with the keen eye of a military analyst. His observations become the blueprint for Rama's war campaign, every insight a step closer to victory. When Hanuman meets Sita, held captive in Ravana's palace, he does not simply offer words of comfort; he acts as a diplomat, providing hope while remaining grounded in the reality of their situation. His message is as much a promise of rescue as it is a strategy to keep Sita's resolve unbroken—a delicate balance of empathy and realism that marks him as more than just a messenger.

It is in moments like these that Hanuman's true genius shines through. For all his legendary strength, it is his understanding of the human heart, his ability to read emotions and motives, that sets him apart as a leader. In a world where battles were often won with might, Hanuman's victories were those of the mind— fought in the shadows of council chambers, in whispered words beneath the trees of Ashoka Vatika, and in the unyielding resolve of a diplomat who knew when to speak softly and when to act decisively.

This book seeks to explore Hanuman not as a distant, mythic figure, but as a living embodiment of strategic brilliance and diplomatic finesse. It is a story that transcends time, offering lessons that are as relevant in today's boardrooms and negotiation tables as they were in the war-torn landscapes of ancient Lanka. Through his story, we will uncover the timeless principles of leadership, diplomacy, and strategy—principles that prove that true power lies not in physical strength alone, but in the wisdom to guide it.

Hanuman's tale is, at its core, a meditation on the power of balance. He could be as gentle as the breeze or as fierce as the storm. He understood that diplomacy and strategy were not signs of weakness, but the marks of a mind that could see the entire chessboard, anticipating moves far ahead of time. His life teaches us that strength without wisdom is chaos, and that true mastery lies in knowing when to wield the sword and when to extend a hand.

In the following pages, we will walk alongside Hanuman through the pivotal moments of his journey—moments that reveal his uncanny ability to blend strategy with compassion, to find paths through the most tangled dilemmas, and to remain steadfast in his mission even when the odds seemed insurmountable. We will see how his influence turned the tides of war, how his counsel shaped the decisions of kings, and how his presence transformed the lives of those around him.

This is the story of Hanuman, the diplomat, the strategist, the tactician. A story of intellect as much as of devotion, of subtlety as much as of strength. As we embark on this journey through his life, let us discover a Hanuman whose wisdom echoes through the ages, reminding us that the greatest victories are often those that begin with a single, thoughtful word.

Chapter 1

ORIGINS OF WISDOM

Key Takeaways

- *Unconventional Learning*: Hanuman learning while flying alongside Surya's chariot. Like Khan Academy founder Sal Khan, who started by tutoring his cousin online and built one of the world's largest free education platforms from his closet-turned-office

- *Demanding Mentorship*: Surya's challenging teaching style. Like Serena Williams' father Richard Williams' tough training methods, pushing her to become a tennis legend through unconventional and demanding coaching

- *Balanced Development*: Hanuman balancing strength with wisdom. Like Bill Gates combining technical expertise with strategic philanthropy, evolving from a tech genius to a global health leader

- *Deep Understanding vs Memorization*: Surya testing Hanuman through riddles Like SpaceX's interview process using problem-solving scenarios instead of traditional questions to hire engineers who can think creatively

- *Pushing Past Comfort*: Hanuman flying to the sun despite the heat. Like Malala Yousafzai continuing to advocate for girls' education despite facing life-threatening opposition, showing courage beyond her years

The sun rose over the lush green hills of Kishkindha, casting its golden light across a forest that had yet to awaken to its full splendor. Birds sang the first notes of morning, and the gentle breeze whispered through the trees. Amidst this serene beauty, a young Hanuman sat cross-legged beneath a towering banyan tree, his eyes closed, his mind deep in contemplation. Even as a child, there was an intensity about him, a curiosity that reached beyond the playful bounds of childhood. He sought to understand not just the world around him, but the world within.

Born to Anjana and the wind god Vayu, Hanuman possessed a unique blend of physical prowess and divine energy. From an early age, his strength and agility set him apart, but it was his insatiable thirst for knowledge that truly distinguished him. It wasn't enough for Hanuman to merely leap from treetops or race the wind—he wanted to know why the wind blew and how the trees spoke in their silent sway. And so, even before his legend as a warrior began, Hanuman embarked on a different journey, one of the mind and the spirit.

Hanuman's mother, Anjana, encouraged this quest for understanding. She would tell him stories of great sages, of the ancient texts that held secrets of the universe, and of Surya, the Sun God, whose radiance illuminated both the heavens and the depths of knowledge. It was from these stories that Hanuman developed a reverence for Surya, seeing him not just as a giver of light but as a keeper of hidden wisdom. The young Hanuman, with the boundless energy of youth, decided that he would seek out Surya himself, not merely to bask in his warmth, but to become his disciple.

One morning, Hanuman made up his mind. With a single leap that shook the earth, he propelled himself into the sky, hurtling towards the sun. As he ascended, he felt the searing heat of Surya's rays, but he pressed on, driven by a desire that burned even brighter. When he finally reached Surya's chariot, the great deity looked upon the small, determined figure with curiosity.

"Why do you come to me, young one?" Surya asked, his voice a booming echo across the heavens.

Hanuman, unperturbed by the Sun God's formidable presence, folded his hands in respectful greeting. "I come seeking knowledge, O Surya Deva. I wish to learn from you—the scriptures, the secrets of the cosmos, the wisdom that flows through time itself. Will you be my guru?"

Surya smiled, but there was a challenge in his eyes. "You wish to learn from me, but I am always moving. I cannot pause my journey across the sky, not even for a moment. How will you keep up?"

Hanuman's eyes sparkled with the thrill of the challenge. "I will fly alongside you, O Deva, and I will learn while I keep pace with your chariot."

Surya raised an eyebrow, intrigued by this fearless youth. "Very well. But understand, knowledge is not given freely. You must prove yourself worthy."

And thus began a journey like no other. Hanuman flew alongside Surya's chariot, soaring through the sky from dawn until dusk, absorbing the teachings of his celestial guru. Surya instructed him in the ancient scriptures—the Vedas, the Upanishads, and the Puranas—filling Hanuman's mind with the hymns and rhythms that held the essence of creation. But the lessons did not stop there. Surya revealed the mysteries of time, the cycles of birth and rebirth, the balance of creation and destruction. Hanuman listened, questioned, and pondered, never losing a step as he kept pace with Surya's unceasing journey.

One evening, as the sun dipped towards the horizon, Surya decided to test his student. He presented Hanuman with a series of riddles, each more intricate than the last, designed to test the depth of his understanding. Surya's first riddle was simple, yet profound, like the first drop of rain before a storm.

"What is the truth that cannot be spoken, yet must be known?"

Hanuman closed his eyes, allowing the question to sink into his being. After a moment, he answered, his voice calm as the evening breeze. "The truth is the self, O Surya Deva. It is that which exists before words, the silence that speaks within. It cannot be described, yet it is known to those who seek it within their hearts."

Surya nodded approvingly, but his expression remained stern. "And what is it that always moves yet remains unchanged?"

Hanuman furrowed his brow, feeling the depth of the question. He glanced at the sun's reflection upon the ocean far below, then looked back at Surya. "It is time, O Deva. Time moves forward, ever-changing, yet the essence of time remains the same—an endless flow that binds the universe together."

Surya's stern facade softened, and he allowed a smile to break through. But the final challenge awaited, a question that tested not only Hanuman's mind but his very understanding of life's duality.

"What is the greatest strength and the greatest weakness of a leader?"

Hanuman pondered this, the sun's rays bathing him in their fading glow. He thought of the kings and sages he had heard of in his mother's stories, of the choices they made and the burdens they bore. And then, with a clarity that cut through all uncertainty, he answered.

"Compassion, O Surya Deva. It is a leader's greatest strength, for it binds him to his people, makes him just, and earns their trust. Yet it can also be his greatest weakness, for it can cloud judgment and lead him to sacrifice too much. A true leader must balance the heart with the mind, knowing when to yield and when to stand firm."

Surya, hearing this, was silent for a long moment, the golden light of dusk casting long shadows across the sky. Then he nodded, a gesture not just of approval but of deep respect. "You have learned well, Hanuman. You have mastered the scriptures, but more importantly, you have understood the nature of wisdom itself. From this day forth, you are not just my student—you are a seeker of truth, a guide for others, and a protector of dharma."

With this blessing, Hanuman's journey with Surya came to a close, but it was only the beginning of his path as a thinker and a strategist. He returned to the earth with a mind sharpened by the sun's fire, ready to face challenges not only with strength but with insight. The lessons he learned in the sky would shape his every decision, guiding him in moments when force alone would fail.

As Hanuman stood upon the earth once more, the stars above twinkling in approval, he realized that true power lay not in the strength of his limbs but in the strength of his mind and heart. And so, he prepared to use this newfound wisdom to navigate the complexities of a world where battles were fought not only with weapons, but with words and ideas.

In the days to come, when the trials of kings and the fate of nations would rest upon his shoulders, it would be this wisdom—born of Surya's light—that would illuminate his path, helping him see the world not as it was, but as it could be.

"Diplomacy is not about winning hearts through persuasion alone but about igniting a shared purpose in the shadows of distrust, where hope dares to bloom."

– Dr. Lal Bhatia

Chapter 2

THE DIPLOMAT EMERGES - HANUMAN AND SUGRIVA

Key Takeaways

- *Building Trust Through Common Ground:* Hanuman connecting Rama and Sugriva by highlighting their shared experiences of loss and exile. Like when Howard Schultz returned to Starbucks as CEO in 2008 during the financial crisis, he united employees by emphasizing their shared struggles and common goal of saving the company. He closed stores for training and openly discussed company challenges, building trust through transparency and shared purpose.

- *Strategic Mediation:* Hanuman's careful approach to introducing Rama to Sugriva, acknowledging fears while offering hope.

Like Tony Blair's role in the Good Friday Agreement (1998), where he carefully mediated between opposing Northern Ireland factions. Like Hanuman, he acknowledged both sides' fears and past traumas while presenting a vision of mutual benefit through peace.

- *Risk Assessment in Alliance Building:* Hanuman's advice to Sugriva about calculated risk-taking in trusting Rama. Like Disney's Bob Iger's acquisition of Pixar in 2006. Despite the huge risk ($7.4 billion), Iger recognized the potential for mutual growth. He carefully managed Steve Jobs' initial skepticism, similar to how Hanuman managed Sugriva's doubts.

- *Power of Effective Communication:* Hanuman's careful choice of words and timing in presenting the alliance opportunity. Mary Barra's communication strategy during GM's ignition switch crisis (2014). Like Hanuman, she chose words carefully, acknowledged past failures, and focused on building trust through transparent communication and action-backed promises.

- *Creating Win-Win Solutions:* Hanuman's ability to show how both Rama and Sugriva could benefit from alliance. Like Microsoft and OpenAI's partnership, where Satya Nadella structured a deal benefiting both companies: OpenAI got computing resources and funding, while Microsoft gained AI technology access. Like Hanuman's diplomacy, this partnership was built on mutual benefit rather than dominance.

The sun hung high over the dense forests of Kishkindha, casting dappled light through the thick canopy. The air was thick with the scents of wildflowers, and a gentle breeze carried the murmurs of a hidden world—one where exiled kings plotted revenge and an ancient kingdom lay in ruin. Amidst this tangled wilderness, Hanuman moved like a shadow, his keen senses attuned to the tensions simmering between the trees. Today, his mission was not one of strength or stealth, but of words— words that could forge alliances, bridge mistrust, and unite hearts against a common enemy.

Sugriva, the exiled king of the vanaras, had been living in fear, hiding from his powerful brother, Vali, who had usurped his throne. Sugriva's followers had dwindled, his confidence eroded by years of living on the edge of survival. Yet in him, Hanuman saw a spark—potential that could be kindled into a flame, but only with the right guidance. Sugriva's kingdom lay in disarray, but his heart still beat with a desire for justice, and Hanuman believed that justice could be the foundation of a new alliance— one that might turn the tide of fate itself.

Meanwhile, in the distant reaches of the forest, Hanuman had encountered two strangers wandering in search of Sugriva. Clad in simple garments of ascetics, yet bearing the poise and aura of kings, they were Lord Rama and his brother, Lakshmana— warriors in exile, seeking help in finding Sita, Rama's beloved, who had been abducted by the demon king Ravana. As Hanuman listened to their story, he saw the convergence of two paths, each shaped by loss and longing, yet holding the promise of renewal if guided towards a common goal.

It was in this moment of realization that Hanuman knew his task: to bring Rama and Sugriva together, to transform their individual struggles into a unified cause. But he also understood that trust, once broken, is not easily rebuilt, and that the hearts of wounded men do not open readily to strangers. This would require more than an introduction—it would require the delicate art of persuasion, a dance between sincerity and pragmatism.

Hanuman approached Sugriva at the foot of Rishyamuka Hill, where the exiled king sat beneath the shade of an ancient tree, surrounded by the last remnants of his loyal followers. Sugriva's face bore the weight of his years in hiding, but his eyes still held the embers of a king's spirit. When he saw Hanuman approach, his expression softened, for he trusted Hanuman as both advisor and friend.

"Sugriva," Hanuman began, his voice steady but warm, "I have met two noble princes in the forest. They are exiles like you, seeking refuge and allies in their quest to rescue one most dear to them. One of them is Lord Rama, whose valor is unmatched and whose purpose is true. He could be the ally you need to reclaim your throne and end your days of hiding."

Sugriva's brow furrowed, suspicion shadowing his face. "An ally, you say? Or another who would use me for his own ends? I have been betrayed before, Hanuman. Why should I trust these strangers?"

Hanuman nodded, acknowledging Sugriva's fears. "Your caution is not misplaced, my friend. But consider this—Rama's loss mirrors your own. His kingdom has been taken from him, his wife is held captive, and his heart burns with the same fire for justice that you hold. He does not seek dominion over Kishkindha; he seeks only your strength to find Sita, as you seek his to defeat Vali. Together, you could restore what was taken from both of you."

Sugriva remained silent, his gaze fixed on the distant horizon where the sun dipped towards twilight. Hanuman sensed his hesitation, the weight of past betrayals pulling against the lure of hope. And so, he spoke again, this time with the voice of a friend who understood the depths of his doubts.

"Trust is a risk, Sugriva. But not all risks are the same. Rama's actions, not merely his words, will reveal his heart. Allow me to bring him to you—speak with him, look into his eyes, and judge for yourself. If you see falsehood, I will stand by your side, and we will turn him away. But if you see truth, then we will have gained a powerful ally. The choice, as always, is yours."

Sugriva looked at Hanuman, and in that moment, the tension broke. He saw not just a messenger, but a mediator who understood his fears yet believed in the possibilities beyond them. With a slow nod, he agreed, though caution still tempered his voice. "Bring them, Hanuman. But know this—if they come with deceit, I will not be fooled again."

With Sugriva's reluctant assent, Hanuman set off into the forest, returning to Rama and Lakshmana with a message that carried both hope and uncertainty. As he led them through the dense foliage towards Rishyamuka Hill, Hanuman's thoughts raced ahead, considering the words that might bridge the gap between these two exiled kings. He knew that this meeting could shape the fate of kingdoms, and every word spoken would matter.

When they arrived, Sugriva stood waiting, his stance rigid with a king's pride yet softened by the shadows of his years in exile. Rama, with his noble bearing and calm demeanor, approached with deference, recognizing the pain that lay behind Sugriva's guarded eyes. Hanuman stepped between them, acting as the thread that would weave their fates together.

"Sugriva, this is Lord Rama, who seeks your friendship, not as a master but as an equal in a shared cause," Hanuman began, his voice carrying the sincerity of one who believed in the bond he was trying to forge. "He offers you his strength, his bow, and his word that he will aid you in your rightful claim to Kishkindha. And in return, he seeks only your help in finding his beloved Sita."

Rama stepped forward, bowing slightly in respect, and spoke with a voice that was steady yet tinged with the grief he carried. "Sugriva, I know the pain of loss, the sting of exile. But I believe that together, we can turn our suffering into strength. I ask not for your loyalty without proving mine. Let me aid you, and judge me by my deeds."

Sugriva studied Rama for a long moment, the silence thick with unspoken thoughts. But in that silence, Hanuman's earlier words echoed in his mind—words that urged him to look beyond his fear, to see the potential in the alliance that lay before him. At last, Sugriva extended his hand, the gesture tentative but genuine.

"If your heart is true, Rama, then I will stand by your side, as you shall stand by mine. Let us cast out the shadows that have haunted us both," Sugriva said, his voice cracking with the weight of his decision. "May this be the beginning of a bond that no force can break."

Rama clasped Sugriva's hand, sealing the alliance, and a sense of relief rippled through Hanuman. He knew that the road ahead would be fraught with battles and trials, but this moment was a victory in its own right—proof that even amidst the darkness of loss, a spark of trust could ignite the flame of hope.

As the sun dipped below the horizon, casting the forest in shades of twilight, Hanuman stood quietly to the side, allowing Rama and Sugriva to speak of their plans. He watched as trust began to take root, slowly but surely, between two men who had lost much but found a common purpose. In that moment, Hanuman understood that the true power of diplomacy lay not in bending wills but in offering a vision that others could believe in—a vision of strength through unity, of battles won not just by arms but by hearts aligned.

The diplomat in Hanuman had emerged, and with it, a new chapter in the story of the world's fate was set into motion.

Chapter 3

JOURNEY TO LANKA - STRATEGIC PLANNING AND RECONNAISSANCE

Key Takeaways

- *Strategic Intelligence Gathering:* Hanuman's careful observation of Lanka's defenses, routines, and vulnerabilities. Like how Samsung's market research team studied Apple's retail operations in the early 2010s. They analyzed everything from store layouts to customer service approaches, leading to the successful launch of Samsung Experience stores that helped them compete effectively in the premium retail space.

- *Leadership Psychology Assessment:* Hanuman's analysis of Ravana's psychology, noticing the doubt behind his confident façade. Like Reed Hastings' insight into Blockbuster's leadership psychology during Netflix's early days. He recognized their overconfidence in the traditional rental model and their hidden fears about digital transition, which helped Netflix position itself strategically for the streaming revolution.

- *Covert Operations and Adaptability.* Hanuman's ability to change forms and move undetected through enemy territory. Like how Satya Nadella transformed Microsoft's approach to competition. Instead of maintaining the company's historically aggressive stance, he adopted a more adaptable strategy, forming partnerships with former rivals like Linux and appearing on Apple's stages - showing how modern leaders can "change form" to navigate competitive landscapes.

- *Identifying Structural Weaknesses.* Hanuman's observation of gaps in Lanka's defense system and patrol patterns. Like how Discord identified and exploited weaknesses in Skype's market position (2015-2018). They recognized that Skype's corporate focus left gamers underserved, leading to Discord's successful targeting of this gap and eventual dominance in gaming communications.

- *Information as Strategic Power.* Hanuman gathering intelligence that could "break a kingdom." Like how WhatsApp's founders identified weaknesses in the traditional SMS market. By gathering data on user dissatisfaction with carrier messaging costs and limitations, they built a service that eventually disrupted the entire telecommunications industry's messaging revenue model, leading to a $19 billion acquisition by Facebook.

The ocean stretched vast and unyielding before Hanuman, its endless waves glinting like liquid gold beneath the sun's fading light. From the edge of the mainland, Hanuman surveyed the waters that separated him from Lanka, a kingdom of shadows and secrets. It was a daunting distance, but not for the physical challenge it posed; for Hanuman, this journey was not merely one of strength but of strategy—of stealth, observation, and the art of turning knowledge into power.

As he prepared to make the leap across the sea, Hanuman took a moment to quiet his mind. He thought of Rama's somber gaze when he entrusted him with this mission, the hope that lingered in Lakshmana's eyes. This was not simply a reconnaissance—this was a mission to peel back the layers of mystery surrounding the demon king Ravana, to learn the lay of the land, the pulse of the enemy, and the vulnerabilities that could one day turn the tide of war.

With a deep breath, Hanuman drew upon the powers gifted to him by his divine lineage, his body swelling with energy as he invoked the strength of the wind, his father's domain. With a powerful thrust, he launched himself into the air, soaring above the churning waves like an arrow loosed from a celestial bow. The wind roared in his ears, carrying whispers of distant lands, and the ocean below seemed to part in awe of his passage. As he soared, Hanuman's mind remained sharp, already beginning to form a plan for the task ahead.

When at last Lanka's dark silhouette appeared on the horizon, its spires rising like jagged teeth against the evening sky, Hanuman slowed his flight, becoming a shadow against the fading twilight. He landed softly on a secluded beach, hidden from view by the thick foliage that fringed the island. For a moment, he crouched low among the trees, his breath blending with the rhythm of the waves. The air was thick with a strange, intoxicating scent, the scent of a land rich with magic and menace. It was a place where every shadow could hide a threat, where every whisper might carry to ears eager to betray.

But Hanuman was not daunted. He moved through the dense undergrowth with the silence of a stalking panther, his mind already assessing the lay of the land. The island's outer defenses, he noted, were formidable—a series of watchtowers patrolled by demon sentinels, their eyes sharp with suspicion. But there were gaps too, in the timing of the patrols, in the shadows where the dense canopy hid the moonlight. These gaps would prove useful for the day when Rama's forces would come, but for now, they were Hanuman's gateway into the heart of Lanka.

He slipped past the sentries, blending into the shadows like a wisp of smoke, making his way toward the city's core. As he drew closer, the jungle gave way to cobblestone streets, illuminated by flickering lanterns. Hanuman observed the bustling markets, where demons bartered strange wares, and the guards that prowled the city's perimeter, their movements precise but predictable. He noted the arrangement of the fortifications, the positions of the barracks, and the routes that would allow the swiftest retreat if discovered. Every detail was etched into his mind, a map that would guide Rama's army when the time came.

But the true heart of his mission lay within the walls of Ravana's palace, a fortress of black stone that loomed over the city like a malevolent mountain. Hanuman knew that if he were to gather the intelligence that mattered most, he would have to enter those walls, to see for himself the man who had taken Sita and hidden her away from the world. He would have to learn not only the defenses that protected Ravana but the very mind of the demon king himself.

Cloaking himself in the guise of a tiny cat, Hanuman slipped through the palace gates, moving with the silent grace of a creature native to the shadows. Inside, the halls of the palace were a labyrinth of gleaming floors and towering columns, adorned with tapestries that depicted the conquests of Ravana, his victories etched in blood and fire. Servants moved through the halls with lowered eyes, while guards in polished armor stood at every junction, their expressions grim.

Hanuman observed all this, taking note of the layout, the patterns of movement, the placement of weapons and traps. Yet, he also saw signs of tension—guards who whispered nervously among themselves, servants who moved with a hurried fear. It was clear that even within this fortress of power, the shadow of Rama's looming presence had begun to sow unease.

He made his way deeper into the palace, slipping past rooms filled with treasures beyond imagination, until he reached a vast chamber where Ravana's throne stood. It was there, in the shadow of the demon king's seat of power, that Hanuman paused to observe.

Ravana sat upon his throne, his many heads adorned with crowns that glimmered in the torchlight, each face reflecting a different emotion—anger, pride, calculation, and a cold, detached wisdom. Hanuman listened as Ravana spoke with his advisors, his voice a deep rumble that filled the chamber.

"We will crush them," Ravana declared, a confident smile curving his lips. "Let Rama come to Lanka. Let him see the might of my legions, the impenetrable walls of this city. His army will shatter like waves against a cliff."

Yet even as Ravana spoke, Hanuman caught a flicker of uncertainty in the demon king's eyes—a fleeting shadow that betrayed the doubt he sought to hide. Hanuman realized that Ravana's bravado masked a deeper fear, a fear that Rama's resolve might match his own, that perhaps the threads of destiny were shifting in ways even Ravana could not control.

Hanuman committed every word to memory, knowing that this insight into Ravana's mind was as valuable as any map or battle plan. He could see the cracks in the armor of Ravana's confidence, the places where words might strike deeper than swords, where a calculated move could unravel the demon king's composure. But even more, he saw the desperation that drove Ravana to hold onto Sita, not merely as a prisoner, but as a symbol of his power over fate itself.

Having gathered all he needed, Hanuman retreated from the palace, slipping through the shadows as easily as he had come. But before he left the city, he sought out the place where Sita was kept, her presence a quiet beacon amidst the darkness. In a secluded grove known as Ashoka Vatika, he found her, seated beneath a tree, her face pale with sorrow yet unbroken in spirit. From a hidden vantage point, Hanuman watched, memorizing her surroundings, the guards posted nearby, the expressions of hope and despair that flickered across her face.

He did not yet reveal himself to her, knowing that the time was not right. But he whispered a silent promise into the night air, a promise that soon, she would not be alone. For now, his mission was to return with the knowledge that could change the course of this war, to bring back a map not just of Lanka's physical terrain but of its vulnerabilities and fears.

As Hanuman leapt back across the ocean, his mind churned with plans and possibilities. He had seen the strengths of Lanka, but more importantly, he had seen its weaknesses—its reliance on the illusion of invincibility, its leader's hubris, and the quiet hope that still lingered in the captive heart of Sita.

When he touched down on the shores of the mainland once more, the night sky above him was alive with stars, each one a reminder of the countless paths that lay ahead. Hanuman knew that the journey to victory would not be simple, but he also knew that knowledge was the most powerful weapon they now possessed. And he, the scout and strategist, had returned with the knowledge that could break a kingdom.

In the days to come, as he recounted his findings to Rama and Lakshmana, Hanuman's voice carried the weight of his mission, the certainty that they could turn the tide against Ravana. He spoke not only of walls and warriors but of minds and motives, of the moments where silence could speak louder than roars.

This was the beginning of a new phase in the war—a phase where words and ideas could shift the balance as surely as any sword. And in this new phase, Hanuman knew, his role as a strategist and a diplomat would prove to be as crucial as his strength.

Chapter 4

MEETING SITA - A DIPLOMAT'S TOUCH

Key Takeaways

- *Empathetic Communication in Crisis:* Hanuman's careful approach to Sita, understanding her emotional state before delivering his message. Like Indra Nooyi's leadership during PepsiCo's transformation (2006-2018). When announcing major organizational changes, she used personal letters to employees and face-to-face meetings, acknowledging their fears while presenting a vision of hope, similar to how Hanuman approached Sita with both empathy and honesty.

- *Building Trust Through Tangible Proof:* Hanuman showing Rama's ring as proof of his authenticity. Like Airbnb's response to the 2020 pandemic crisis. CEO Brian Chesky didn't just make promises - he backed them with concrete actions, including a $250 million host support fund and clear safety protocols, providing tangible proof of the company's commitment to its community.

- *Balancing Hope with Realism*: Hanuman's honest assessment of challenges while maintaining hope. Like Anne Mulcahy's communication during Xerox's near-bankruptcy (2000-2002). Like Hanuman, she was honest about the company's dire situation while maintaining hope, telling employees: "We're in a hole but we know how to get out." Her balanced approach helped rally employees during the successful turnaround.

- *Strategic Timing in Communication*: Hanuman choosing the right moment to reveal himself after careful observation. Like Tim Cook's handling of Apple's transition from Intel to Apple Silicon (2020). The announcement was carefully timed after years of preparation, with a clear two-year transition plan that provided certainty while acknowledging challenges ahead.

- *Building Resilience Through Connection*: Hanuman strengthening Sita's resolve by connecting her to a larger purpose. Like Dan Price of Gravity Payments during the 2020 crisis. When faced with a 50% revenue drop, he transparently shared the company's situation with employees, who voluntarily took pay cuts to avoid layoffs. By connecting individual sacrifices to the company's survival, he strengthened collective resilience.

The night in Lanka was thick with silence, a silence that seemed to smother even the whispers of the trees in Ashoka Vatika. A crescent moon hung low in the sky, its pale light casting long shadows over the ancient grove. The air was heavy with the scent of blooming flowers, but beneath their fragrance lurked the cold steel of despair. In the heart of this garden, amidst the dark canopy of leaves, Sita sat alone, her eyes turned toward the distant stars, searching for a sign, a glimmer of hope that had evaded her for too long.

It was here, in this place of both beauty and sorrow, that Hanuman finally revealed himself. After days of observing from the shadows, watching Sita's quiet suffering, he knew that the moment had come to step forward—not as a warrior, but as a messenger, a bringer of hope. He approached her with the careful tread of a diplomat who understands the delicate nature of his mission, aware that a single misstep could deepen the cracks in her resolve.

Hanuman took a moment to study her before making himself known. She was a picture of grace even in captivity, her face pale but resolute, her shoulders carrying the weight of her suffering with a dignity that moved him. Yet beneath that outer calm, he sensed the weariness of a heart that had fought for too long against the darkness. He saw the way her hands clutched a small piece of cloth—perhaps a fragment of the past, a memory of Rama—and he knew that his words would need to touch that very thread of longing that kept her anchored to hope.

He began by speaking softly, allowing his voice to blend with the murmur of the night. "Sita, O noble queen, do not be afraid. I am a friend, a messenger sent by one who holds you dearer than life itself."

Sita turned, startled, her eyes wide with a mixture of fear and wonder. Hanuman stepped into the moonlight, bowing low with the reverence of one who understands the sanctity of her presence. He saw her suspicion, the guarded look in her eyes, but also the faint flicker of something else—an ember of hope that had long been buried beneath layers of doubt.

"Who are you, and how do you know my name?" she asked, her voice steady despite the tremor in her hands.

Hanuman straightened, his expression gentle yet firm, the words he had rehearsed in his mind flowing with the grace of a river. "I am Hanuman, a servant of Lord Rama, who has crossed the ocean in search of you. He has not forgotten you, my lady. His heart beats with your name, his thoughts are filled with your memory, and he seeks you with a fervor that no distance can diminish."

As he spoke, he watched Sita's face closely, noting the way her breath caught, the way her eyes softened at the sound of Rama's name. But he knew that words alone could not erase the months of fear and uncertainty that had haunted her. He would need to do more than speak—he would need to build a bridge between her pain and her hope, one step at a time.

Hanuman took out a small signet ring, Rama's ring, and held it out to her, the silver catching the moon's light. "This is a token from him," he said, his voice dropping to a near-whisper. "A sign of his love and his promise. He has sent me to tell you that he will come for you, that this separation is not the end, but a trial that will soon be overcome."

Sita reached for the ring with trembling hands, cradling it as if it were the most fragile of treasures. Tears welled in her eyes, but they were not the tears of despair—they were the tears of a heart that had found a crack in the darkness. She clutched the ring to her chest, her voice breaking as she spoke. "Does he truly remember me? Does he still hold hope, even after all this time?"

Hanuman knelt before her, his tone imbued with the empathy of a confidant. "My lady, there has not been a single moment when he has forgotten you. His every breath is a prayer for your safety, his every step a journey towards reuniting with you. He has formed an alliance with the vanaras, led by Sugriva, and even now prepares to march upon Lanka. But he knows that strength alone cannot prevail without hope. That is why he sent me, to remind you that you are not alone in your suffering."

He paused, letting his words settle like the gentle fall of rain on parched earth. Sita's expression shifted, the harsh lines of worry easing slightly, but still, shadows lingered in her gaze. Hanuman understood that even hope could be a painful thing to embrace when one had grown accustomed to despair. He adjusted his tone, blending reassurance with pragmatism.

"But I will not lie to you, Sita. The road ahead is not without peril. Ravana's strength is formidable, and his forces are vast. The path to your freedom will be fraught with battles and sacrifices.

Yet, I have seen Rama's determination, and I have seen the cracks in Ravana's armor. Victory is not beyond reach, but it requires your strength as well. Can you find it in your heart to endure a little longer, knowing that the dawn is near?"

Sita studied Hanuman, her expression a mixture of vulnerability and a rising courage. In his words, she sensed not the empty promises of comfort, but the honesty of one who respected her strength. For the first time in months, she allowed herself to imagine a future beyond her captivity, to picture the day when she might once again stand by Rama's side. A tentative smile touched her lips, and she nodded, though her voice remained fragile.

"I will endure, Hanuman. I will hold onto this hope you have brought me, as I hold this ring. Tell Rama that I will await his coming, no matter how long it takes."

Hanuman bowed his head, a deep sense of satisfaction filling his chest. He had not merely delivered a message—he had rekindled a spirit that had nearly been extinguished, offering a glimpse of light in the darkness. But he knew that his mission was not yet complete. He spoke again, a note of urgency creeping into his tone.

"Sita, there is one more thing you must know. I have seen the guards, the defenses that hold you here. I can return to Rama with the knowledge of their positions, of the routes he must take to reach you. But you must remain vigilant. Do not let Ravana's threats shake your resolve. Your strength will be the anchor that guides Rama's heart in these dark times."

Sita nodded, and for the first time since his arrival, he saw a glimmer of the queen she had been—the unwavering strength that had made her the heart of Rama's kingdom. Hanuman felt a swell of respect for this woman who, despite the shadows that surrounded her, had not allowed her spirit to be fully broken.

Before taking his leave, Hanuman folded his hands in a deep gesture of respect, his voice carrying the warmth of a promise. "May your heart remain steady, Sita. The night may seem long, but dawn is certain. And when it comes, it will be Rama's voice that calls you home."

With those words, Hanuman leapt into the shadows once more, slipping through the night with the same silence that had brought him to the garden. He moved quickly, knowing that the time for stealth was nearing its end and the time for battle was approaching. Yet, as he made his way back towards the shores of Lanka, he carried with him a sense of fulfilment. He had seen the spark of hope ignite in Sita's eyes, and he knew that it would burn brightly enough to guide Rama through whatever trials lay ahead.

In the days to come, as Rama prepared to cross the ocean and face the might of Ravana's armies, Hanuman's words to Sita would echo in his mind. They were words that held the promise of reunion, but also the reminder that diplomacy was not only about deals and negotiations—it was about understanding the hearts of those who waited in the darkness and giving them the strength to believe in the dawn.

And in this, Hanuman had proven himself a true diplomat, a master not of courtly intrigue but of the quiet, essential art of building hope amidst despair.

Chapter 5

WAGING PSYCHOLOGICAL WARFARE

Key Takeaways

- *Strategic Self-Exposure:* Hanuman deliberately allowing himself to be captured to deliver his psychological message. Similarly, Elon Musk's calculated "failures" with SpaceX's early rocket launches. By publicly showing these failures and the company's resilience, he transformed potential criticism into a narrative of perseverance, making competitors question their own conservative approaches to innovation.

- *Undermining Authority Through Perception:* Hanuman planting seeds of doubt about Ravana among his followers. Similarly, Netflix's Reed Hastings openly challenging Blockbuster's business model in 2010. By publicly questioning Blockbuster's relevance in the digital age, he not only shook investor confidence in Blockbuster but made their own employees doubt their company's future, accelerating their decline.

- *Power of Public Confrontation:* Hanuman's bold speech in Ravana's court, turning a moment of capture into a demonstration of strength. Similarly, Microsoft's Satya Nadella's 2014 bold move to demonstrate Office on iPad at Apple's event. This unexpected public appearance on a competitor's stage showed Microsoft's confidence and new direction, challenging perceptions of the company as solely Windows-focused.

- *Creating Symbolic Moments:* Hanuman's fiery escape becoming a powerful symbol of defiance. Similarly, Richard Branson's Virgin Galactic flight in July 2021. By flying to space before Jeff Bezos, he created a symbolic moment that challenged Blue Origin's perceived leadership in space tourism, affecting both public perception and investor confidence.

- *Psychological Warfare Through Confidence:* Hanuman's laughter and calm demeanor in the face of threats. Similarly, Apple's Tim Cook handling the FBI iPhone encryption battle in 2016. His calm, unwavering stance in defending user privacy, despite immense pressure, not only strengthened Apple's position but made government agencies reconsider their approach to tech companies' cooperation.

The streets of Lanka hummed with a tense stillness as Hanuman moved through the shadows, his steps slow and deliberate. He had gathered all the intelligence he needed—he knew the layout of Ravana's palace, the positions of his guards, and the corridors of power that kept the demon king's reign intact. But now, as he prepared for the final phase of his mission, Hanuman's thoughts turned to a different kind of battle, one that would not be fought with weapons but with words, with the power to twist perception and plant seeds of doubt.

Hanuman knew that he could slip away, return to Rama with the information he had gathered, and prepare for the inevitable clash between Rama's forces and Ravana's legions. But he also understood the nature of fear, how it could eat away at resolve and spread like wildfire through even the bravest hearts. He saw an opportunity—to confront Ravana directly, to make himself a symbol of Rama's coming wrath, and to shatter the illusion of invincibility that Ravana used to keep his subjects in line. It would be a dangerous gambit, but Hanuman had learned that sometimes, the most strategic move was to place oneself directly in the lion's den.

With a final, resolute breath, Hanuman allowed himself to be seen. He shed the shadows that had hidden him and strode openly through the palace gardens, leaving a trail of broken defenses in his wake. The alarm spread quickly, rippling through the palace like the tolling of a bell, and soon, Hanuman was surrounded by Ravana's guards, their weapons gleaming in the torchlight.

The demons seized him, binding his arms with chains as thick as iron vines, but Hanuman offered no resistance. He could see the confusion in their eyes, the unease at how easily they had captured this figure who had eluded them for so long. They did not know that they were not dragging a prisoner but escorting a player who had already scripted the scene that was about to unfold.

They led him through the grand halls of the palace, past towering statues and walls adorned with gold and ivory, until they reached the throne room. It was a vast chamber, its ceilings disappearing into shadows, and at its center sat Ravana, his ten heads crowned in gold, each face radiating a different expression—fury, disdain, and something that Hanuman recognized as curiosity.

Hanuman's eyes swept the room, noting the expressions of the courtiers who stood in tense silence along the walls. They were used to seeing their king command with absolute authority, to crush defiance with the weight of his power. But today, Hanuman would change the rhythm of this chamber. Today, he would turn the gaze of every demon towards the cracks in Ravana's rule.

The guards forced Hanuman to his knees before Ravana's throne, but he did not bow his head. He met the demon king's gaze with unflinching defiance, a half-smile curling at the corners of his lips. It was a smile that spoke of secrets yet to be revealed, of a game already in motion.

"So, this is the creature that dares to trespass in my kingdom?" Ravana's voice boomed through the hall, each word a thunderclap that echoed against the walls. His many eyes studied Hanuman with a mixture of anger and amusement. "Speak, monkey, before I decide what fate awaits you. Who sent you, and what is your purpose here?"

Hanuman's smile widened, his voice calm but carrying a steel edge that cut through the air. "I come as a messenger, O Ravana, from Lord Rama, the one whose name already stirs whispers in your court. I have crossed your seas, passed through your walls, and entered your palace with a purpose that you cannot stop."

Ravana's expression darkened, his anger bubbling just beneath the surface, but Hanuman pressed on, his voice rising, commanding the attention of every ear in the chamber. "You think yourself invincible, surrounded by your legions and your wealth, but know this, Ravana—your days of tyranny are numbered. Rama's arrows are already aimed at your gates, and the fires of his wrath will consume this city if you do not return Sita. I am but the first ember of a coming blaze."

A murmur rippled through the court, the demons exchanging uneasy glances. Hanuman could see the seed of doubt taking root, spreading like a shadow across the faces of Ravana's advisors. He knew that fear, once planted, was a weed that grew swiftly, wrapping itself around the heart until it choked out all certainty.

Ravana, sensing the shift in his court, leaned forward, his eyes narrowing into slits. "You speak boldly for a captive. Do you think I fear your words, or your so-called lord? You are in my power now, and you will die for your insolence."

Hanuman met Ravana's threat with laughter, a sound that echoed through the chamber like a clash of cymbals. It was not the laughter of mockery, but of one who knew more than he revealed, who held the advantage even when surrounded. "Kill me if you wish, Ravana, but it will not silence the truth I have spoken. My death will only prove that you fear Rama's approach, that you fear the power he wields."

He shifted his gaze to the courtiers, letting his words find their mark. "Ask yourselves, O demons of Lanka, why your king rages at the mention of Rama's name. Ask yourselves why he hides behind his walls and chains, while Rama walks with the gods. Is it because he fears no one—or because he knows that his time is running out?"

The silence that followed was palpable, a silence that pressed against Ravana's pride like a blade. Hanuman saw the way the courtiers shifted, their expressions uncertain, their loyalty shaken by the question he had placed in their minds. Ravana's anger flared, and with a swift motion, he ordered Hanuman's execution—but in his haste, he had already revealed his fear.

Yet Hanuman knew that his final move was still to come. As the guards dragged him away, he called out in a voice that rang through the hall like a trumpet's blast. "Remember my words, Ravana! The sun does not set without casting shadows, and your pride will be your downfall! Return Sita, or face the wrath that will sweep across this land like a storm!"

The chamber buzzed with tension as Hanuman was hauled outside, his chains clanking with each step. But in the faces of those who watched him, he saw something that told him he had achieved his aim—a flicker of doubt, a question that would fester long after he was gone. He had planted fear like a poison in Ravana's court, a fear that would gnaw at the edges of their confidence, turning their certainty into a brittle shell.

As he was brought to the courtyard where the pyre awaited, Hanuman remained calm, his mind already spinning with the next phase of his plan. He allowed the flames to touch his bound hands, but he did not feel the searing heat as an ending. Instead, he let the fire consume the ropes that held him, and with a mighty leap, he rose above the blaze, his body alight with flame, becoming a figure of terror silhouetted against the night sky.

From the palace walls, the demons watched in awe and horror as Hanuman, burning like a comet, took to the air. His voice echoed over the city, a final declaration that carried both warning and promise. "Lanka will burn if you do not heed my words! Rama's strength is as unyielding as the fire that now scorches your pride! I am but the beginning—he is the end that you cannot escape!"

With those words, Hanuman soared into the night, leaving behind a city gripped by the flames of both fire and fear. As he flew back across the ocean, he knew that he had set the stage for the battles to come, that he had transformed himself from a mere scout into a symbol of the coming storm. He had shown that sometimes, the most potent weapon in a warrior's arsenal is not the sword or the arrow, but the power to shape the thoughts of those who oppose him.

And as the embers of his message smoldered within the palace of Lanka, Ravana himself felt the first chill of uncertainty, a crack in the wall of his arrogance. It was a crack that Hanuman knew Rama would soon widen, with the force of an army and the righteousness of a cause that could not be denied.

"Before you can build something new, sometimes you need to let people see their invincible fortress burn."

– Dr. Lal Bhatia

Chapter 6

THE BURNING OF LANKA - CONTROLLED CHAOS

Key Takeaways

- *Strategic Disruption:* Hanuman's calculated burning of Lanka's key infrastructure (armories, granaries) to weaken the enemy. Similarly, how Netflix strategically disrupted Blockbuster by targeting their revenue streams. Instead of competing directly, Netflix systematically attacked Blockbuster's late fees (which represented 12% of revenue) by introducing their no-late-fees model, effectively burning down a key pillar of their competitor's business model.

- *Symbolic Destruction of Power:* Hanuman burning Ravana's statues to shatter the illusion of invincibility. Similarly, the fall of BlackBerry's market dominance. Apple's iPhone launch didn't just compete with BlackBerry - it symbolically destroyed the notion that physical keyboards were essential for business phones, breaking BlackBerry's aura of corporate invincibility.

- *Controlled Chaos as Strategy.* Hanuman's systematic approach to setting fires across Lanka. Similarly, Amazon's deliberate disruption of traditional retail. Jeff Bezos's strategy of "your margin is my opportunity" systematically targeted different retail sectors, creating controlled chaos in traditional retail while maintaining a clear strategic vision.

- *Breaking Enemy Morale.* Using fire to create panic and uncertainty among Ravana's forces. Similarly, Tesla's impact on traditional automakers. Elon Musk's continuous announcements and achievements in electric vehicles created a psychological impact that shook the confidence of traditional auto manufacturers, making their employees and investors question their future viability.

- *Creating Visible Symbols of Vulnerability.* Making Lanka's burning visible to demonstrate Ravana's vulnerability. Similarly, how Zoom exposed Microsoft's vulnerability during the 2020 pandemic. By becoming the default video conferencing tool despite Microsoft's existing Teams platform, Zoom created a visible demonstration that even tech giants could be outmaneuvered, affecting Microsoft's perceived dominance in enterprise software.

The air in Lanka was heavy with the scent of smoke, mingling with the salt of the sea breeze. The city slept uneasily under the watchful gaze of its sentinels, but in the shadows, a different kind of fire smoldered—one that had been kindled not by chance but by design. Hanuman crouched atop a palace wall, his eyes scanning the sprawl of the city below, his mind turning over the strategy that had brought him to this moment.

In the aftermath of his fiery escape from Ravana's court, he could have left Lanka behind, returning to Rama's camp with the knowledge he had gathered. But as he stood amid the rising tension of Ravana's court, he had seen an opportunity—a chance to strike at the very heart of Lanka's illusion of invincibility, to make a statement that would reverberate through Ravana's kingdom like a thunderclap. The decision to burn Lanka had come to him not as a flash of rage, but as the realization of how fire could become a weapon, one that would turn fear into a force that crippled the enemy from within.

Hanuman moved through the darkened alleys of Lanka with the grace of a shadow, his thoughts precise and focused. He knew that to set the city ablaze was to invite retaliation, but he also knew that sometimes, chaos was the key to disrupting power. Ravana's strength lay not only in his armies but in the belief that his rule was unassailable. If Hanuman could turn the flames against him, if he could light a fire that symbolized the end of that illusion, then the demons would no longer see their king as a shield but as a man whose power could falter.

With this plan in mind, Hanuman sought out the strategic points of the city, his movements guided by the map he had committed to memory. He passed the armories where Ravana's weapons were stockpiled, the barracks where soldiers rested, and the granaries that stored food for times of siege. These were the veins that fed Ravana's war machine, and Hanuman knew that a well-placed flame could turn them from assets into weaknesses.

He gathered dry twigs and oil-soaked rags as he moved, making small, discreet piles that would ignite quickly. Each time he set a flame, he did so with a purpose, letting the fire catch and grow before slipping away into the night. It was a dance of controlled destruction, where every flickering blaze served a calculated aim.

The first fires took hold in the armories, the oil-soaked timbers catching with a roar that shattered the quiet of the night. Flames licked up the walls, consuming the weapons that had been forged to rain down upon Rama's forces. Hanuman watched as the guards rushed to contain the blaze, their shouts mingling with the crackle of burning wood. But even as they fought to douse the flames, new fires sprang up in the barracks and the granaries, spreading panic through the ranks of soldiers who had once believed themselves invincible.

Hanuman's lips curled into a grim smile as he observed the unfolding chaos. He knew that Ravana's warriors would be forced to confront a new reality—that their fortress could be breached, that their control over the land was slipping like sand through their fingers. But more than that, he knew that the sight of flames devouring their strongholds would send a message to Sita, hidden in her garden, and to the people of Lanka who had suffered under Ravana's iron hand. It was a message that Rama's justice was not a distant dream but a force that could reach even the heart of their city.

As the fires spread, their glow painting the sky with a fierce, unearthly light, Hanuman made his way to the palace courtyard, the last place he intended to ignite. It was here that the symbols of Ravana's pride were most visible—statues of the demon king, carved in stone and bronze, towering over the courtyards like silent sentinels. Hanuman paused before one of the statues, his hands resting on the oil-soaked rags he had gathered.

For a moment, he thought of the many faces he had seen in the city—the faces of those who served Ravana out of fear, who saw no way out of the shadow that he cast over their lives. And in that moment, he made his decision. He would burn the symbols of Ravana's power, not merely as an act of destruction but as a beacon to those who longed for something beyond their chains.

With a swift motion, he lit the rags, watching as the flames danced up the base of the statue, turning the bronze into a glowing pillar. He moved from one statue to the next, until a ring of fire encircled the courtyard, each blaze a defiant challenge to the might of Ravana. When the last flame was lit, Hanuman turned and leapt to the palace wall, his silhouette framed by the inferno he had set in motion.

As he stood atop the wall, looking down upon the city, he saw the flames spreading through the night, consuming wood and stone with equal hunger. Yet in the destruction, there was a strange, terrible beauty—a vision of how even the strongest walls could fall when met with a fire that carried the promise of change. Hanuman felt the heat on his face, but he also felt the chill of what this moment represented: a turning point, a shift in power that could not be undone.

Below him, the demons ran to and fro, their cries rising in a cacophony of confusion and terror. Ravana's lieutenants shouted orders, trying to rally their soldiers to fight the flames, but Hanuman knew that they were not fighting fire—they were fighting the fear that had taken root in their hearts. With each flame that rose higher, the certainty of their invincibility burned away, leaving only the raw, searing knowledge that their fortress was no longer impenetrable.

As the fires reached their zenith, Hanuman leapt into the sky, soaring above the city, his form wreathed in the glow of the burning city below. He looked back one last time, his heart heavy but resolute. He saw the chaos he had unleashed, the smoke that now billowed over Lanka, but he also saw the purpose behind it—a purpose that would become clear in the battles to come.

Ravana would view this as an act of war, an affront to his pride that demanded retribution. But in his haste for vengeance, he would be blinded to the true significance of what had happened. Hanuman knew that the fires he had set were not meant to destroy Ravana's city, but to break the spell of fear that held it together, to show that even a lone messenger could defy the might of Lanka.

As he flew back towards the shores of India, Hanuman's thoughts turned to Rama and the coming war. He had struck the first blow, not with a weapon but with a vision of fire that would haunt the dreams of Ravana's warriors. He had shown that sometimes, the path to victory was not in avoiding chaos but in using it as a tool, turning destruction into a sign of resistance that could rally the oppressed and shake the foundations of tyranny.

And as the flames of Lanka faded into the distance behind him, Hanuman felt the weight of his choices settle on his shoulders. He knew that this act would echo through the days to come, shaping the destiny of kingdoms. But he also knew that he had done what needed to be done, that he had lit a fire that could not be extinguished until it had burned through the chains that bound Sita and shattered the illusions that held Lanka in thrall.

It was a fire that would forge a new future, and Hanuman, with his calculated act of defiance, had become its spark.

Chapter 7

THE WAR COUNCIL - STRATEGIC BRILLIANCE

Key Takeaways

- *Turning Enemy Strengths into Weaknesses.* Hanuman using the demons' nighttime advantage against them by adopting their own tactics. Similarly, Apple's iPhone strategy against Nokia in 2007-2010. While Nokia dominated with hardware expertise, Apple turned this strength into a weakness by shifting the battleground to software and user experience, making Nokia's hardware prowess less relevant in the new smartphone era.

- *Asymmetric Warfare Strategy.* Hanuman's use of small, mobile units for guerrilla tactics instead of direct confrontation. Similarly, Airbnb's approach to competing with traditional hotels. Instead of building hotels, they created a distributed network of private accommodations, using their competitors' fixed locations and high overhead as a weakness while maintaining flexibility and lower costs.

- *Terrain-Based Strategy:* Hanuman using the eastern jungle's challenging terrain to their advantage. Similarly, how Discord captured the gaming market by understanding its unique "terrain." Rather than competing on general social media platforms, Discord specifically designed its features for gaming communities' needs, using the specialized environment to their advantage.

- Adaptive Leadership: Hanuman training troops in new tactics rather than relying on traditional warfare methods. Similarly, Microsoft's transformation under Satya Nadella. He retrained the company's workforce to be "cloud-first," adapting their skills from traditional software development to cloud computing, like how Hanuman retrained warriors in new tactics.

- *Strategic Positioning:* Hanuman's placement of hidden units in key locations before the battle. Similarly, how Spotify positioned itself against Apple Music. Instead of competing solely on music library (where Apple was strong), Spotify strategically positioned itself through podcast acquisitions, personalized playlists, and social features, creating multiple points of advantage in areas where Apple wasn't focused.

The sea breeze swept across the makeshift camp where Rama's army had gathered, carrying with it the scent of salt and the distant echo of crashing waves. Tents dotted the sandy shore, their fabric rippling like banners in the wind, while warriors sharpened their weapons and shared hushed conversations, their minds already braced for the battles ahead. Across the water lay Lanka, its once-imposing silhouette now marked by the scars of Hanuman's flames—a city that smoldered with a new, uncertain tension.

Within a large pavilion at the center of the camp, the atmosphere was different—charged with the energy of strategy, calculation, and anticipation. Rama sat at the head of a wooden table, his eyes dark with determination, while his brother Lakshmana and the leaders of the vanara army gathered around him, waiting for the council to begin. And there, standing with an air of quiet confidence, was Hanuman, the architect of the fires that had already begun to change the tide of this war.

As the murmur of conversation faded, Rama turned to Hanuman, his gaze filled with the trust that had grown between them over the course of this journey. "Hanuman," he said, his voice steady, "you have walked the streets of Lanka, seen their fortifications, and tested their strength. Now, we face the challenge of breaking through Ravana's defenses. Tell us—how do we turn our strengths into victory?"

Hanuman nodded, his mind already racing with the possibilities. He had spent the days since his return studying the terrain, observing the movements of the demons along the shoreline, and considering the weaknesses he had glimpsed during his time in Ravana's city. He knew that brute force alone would not be enough to shatter the defenses of a kingdom that had withstood centuries of assault. This would require precision, adaptability, and the element of surprise.

He placed a map of Lanka on the table, the parchment creased with use. Leaning forward, he traced a line along the coast with his finger, his voice calm but laced with a steely edge. "Ravana's forces are strongest along the western shore, where the cliffs provide a natural defense. His troops are concentrated here, expecting a direct assault. But their strength becomes a weakness if we turn it against them. We should strike from the east, where the terrain is more challenging but the defenses are thinner. We can use the cover of the jungle to mask our approach."

Lakshmana nodded thoughtfully, but he furrowed his brow as he studied the map. "That may work for our initial landing, but the demons are known for their night-time raids. They will use the darkness to sow confusion in our ranks. How do we hold our ground when the night is theirs?"

A shadow crossed the faces of those present, a reminder of the demons' reputation for launching swift, devastating attacks under cover of darkness. But Hanuman only smiled, a glint of calculation in his eyes. This was the very challenge he had anticipated, and he had already devised a way to turn it into their advantage.

"Night can be a weapon for those who know how to wield it," Hanuman said, meeting each of their gazes with unflinching confidence. "Ravana's forces rely on the cover of darkness to hide their movements, but it also means that they are not prepared for an enemy that can strike from the shadows as they do. I propose that we use their tactics against them—launching our own ambushes when they least expect it."

He pointed to a series of ravines and dense thickets that ran along the edge of the eastern jungle, places where the landscape itself could become their ally. "We will place small, mobile units here, hidden among the rocks and trees. When the demons attempt their raids, they will find themselves caught in a trap—surrounded on all sides, unable to distinguish friend from foe in the darkness. We will turn their own strategy against them, striking swiftly and then retreating before they can regroup."

Rama listened intently, his expression thoughtful as he weighed Hanuman's words. The plan was bold, requiring precision and discipline from their troops, but it also offered a way to shift the balance of power. He could see how it might work—how they could disrupt the demons' confidence, breaking their rhythm and forcing them to fight on unfamiliar terms.

"It is risky," Lakshmana said, though his voice held a note of respect. "But it could work. If we can keep them off balance, we can weaken their morale before the main assault. What do you think, brother?"

Rama's gaze remained fixed on Hanuman, a hint of a smile tugging at the corners of his lips. "I think Hanuman has seen further into the heart of this battle than we have. If we use the night as he suggests, we turn Ravana's own strengths into his downfall."

With Rama's approval, the plan was set into motion. Over the next days, Hanuman worked closely with the vanara leaders, selecting warriors skilled in guerrilla tactics and training them in the art of ambush. He taught them how to blend with the shadows, to use the cover of the trees and the lay of the land, and to strike without leaving a trace. He showed them how to use the terrain to their advantage, turning each ravine and thicket into a potential trap.

On the eve of the first assault, Hanuman stood with Rama and Lakshmana, watching as their troops moved silently into position. The jungle stretched out before them, dark and impenetrable, but Hanuman's mind saw it as a map of opportunities, each shadow a place where their forces could lie in wait.

As the moon rose high above the canopy, casting a silver light across the landscape, the first wave of demon raiders emerged from the darkness. They moved with confidence, believing the night to be their ally, but as they reached the edge of the jungle, the silence shattered. Hanuman's hidden units sprang into action, striking from the cover of the trees, surrounding the demons and cutting off their retreat.

The night filled with the clash of steel and the cries of battle, but Hanuman's strategy proved its worth. The demons, expecting a scattered and panicked enemy, found themselves facing a foe that moved with precision, appearing and vanishing like ghosts among the trees. Each time the demons regrouped, another ambush awaited them, until the raiders, once so sure of their dominance, were forced into a retreat, their morale broken by the relentless assault.

As dawn broke over the battlefield, Rama's forces emerged from the jungle victorious, their spirits lifted by the success of their first encounter. And though the battle had only just begun, the tide had already begun to shift. Hanuman's plan had done more than repel an attack—it had sent a message to Ravana's forces that the darkness they had once commanded was no longer theirs alone.

That evening, as the war council gathered again, Hanuman spoke quietly with Rama, his voice filled with the calm of one who had seen his plans bear fruit. "This victory is but a foothold, my lord. Ravana will respond with greater force, but now he knows that his tactics are not beyond our reach. We must continue to adapt, to strike where he is unprepared."

Rama clasped Hanuman's shoulder, gratitude and respect shining in his eyes. "You have shown us that victory lies not in strength alone, but in the ability to see beyond the moment, to plan for what lies unseen. With you at our side, I have no doubt that we can overcome whatever challenges lie ahead."

Hanuman nodded, but his thoughts remained focused on the battles to come. He knew that each victory would bring new challenges, that the true test of strategy lay not in a single triumph but in the ability to adapt, to remain one step ahead of an ever-changing enemy. And as he looked out over the horizon, where the sun dipped toward the sea, he saw the shape of the battles yet to come, the opportunities hidden within each risk, and the promise of a war that would be won not just with arms, but with the mind.

For Hanuman, this was the essence of strategy—the ability to see beyond the chaos of the moment, to anticipate the moves of an opponent, and to turn even the smallest advantage into a decisive turning point. It was a lesson he had learned in the shadow of Surya's chariot, and now, in the heart of the war council, it had become the foundation of a plan that could change the fate of kingdoms.

The fires that had burned in Lanka were no longer the only flames that lit the path to victory. Now, they were joined by the sparks of strategy, of foresight, of a vision that saw beyond the battlefield to the possibilities that lay hidden in every shadow. And as Hanuman stood alongside his allies, he knew that this was the battle he had been born to fight—a battle where the mind, as much as the body, would determine the shape of the future.

Chapter 8

RAVANA'S DEFEAT - THE MIND BEHIND THE MUSCLE

Key Takeaways

- *Psychological Warfare Through Perception Management:* Hanuman using divine weapons to shatter the belief in Ravana's invincibility. Similarly, Tesla's impact on traditional automakers. By consistently showcasing advanced technology (like over-the-air updates and Autopilot), Tesla shattered the perceived technological superiority of established car manufacturers, making their customers and investors question their market dominance.

- *Breaking the Leader's Aura:* Targeting Ravana's image of invincibility in front of his troops. Similarly, Apple's 2007 iPhone launch against BlackBerry. Steve Jobs didn't just release a competing product; he systematically demolished BlackBerry's core beliefs about what made a business phone "professional," breaking their leadership aura in the corporate world.

- *Timing Strategic Strikes.* Hanuman waiting for Ravana's frustration to peak before launching the divine weapons attack. Similarly, Netflix's perfectly timed shift to streaming. They waited until broadband penetration reached critical mass before pushing streaming services, timing their strategic pivot to when Blockbuster was most vulnerable and least able to adapt.

- *Exploiting Leadership Weaknesses.* Using Ravana's pride and fear against him. Similarly, how AMD under Lisa Su exploited Intel's manufacturing delays and overconfidence (2018-2021). Su recognized Intel's pride in their manufacturing prowess had become a weakness, and strategically targeted this vulnerability with more nimble third-party manufacturing partnerships.

- *Creating Cascading Doubt.* Making Ravana's troops question their allegiance through demonstrated vulnerability. Similarly, how Zoom exposed Microsoft's vulnerability during the 2020 pandemic. Each successful Zoom meeting in a major corporation created doubt about Microsoft Teams' necessity, causing a cascading effect where even longtime Microsoft-loyal organizations began questioning their traditional software choices.

The battlefield stretched wide beneath the crimson sky, its sands stained with the struggles of days past. War cries and the clash of weapons filled the air, mingling with the dust and the smell of sweat and blood. The forces of Rama and Ravana collided like waves against a cliff, each assault met with fierce resistance, each victory hard-won. And in the heart of this storm, Hanuman stood as both warrior and strategist, his keen mind working tirelessly to turn the tide of this final conflict.

Ravana's army was relentless, a tide of demons whose numbers seemed endless. Yet, Hanuman understood that the true battle lay not just in the strength of arms but in the breaking of wills. As he fought alongside Rama's forces, he saw the patterns that emerged amidst the chaos, the subtle shifts in the morale of both sides. It was in these shifts, these fleeting moments of uncertainty, that he saw the threads that could unravel the power of Lanka's greatest king.

One such moment came after a fierce skirmish near the walls of Lanka, where Rama's forces had managed to push Ravana's army back but at great cost. As the vanara warriors regrouped, Hanuman joined Rama and Lakshmana on a hill overlooking the battlefield, their faces drawn with the strain of the conflict. Below, the fires of battle flickered in the fading light, but in the distance, the dark shape of Ravana's chariot moved like a shadow among shadows.

Rama's face was grim as he surveyed the scene, his bow resting on his knee. "Ravana's forces are strong, and he commands them with unwavering resolve. We have broken through his outer defenses, but his heart remains unyielding. Each victory seems to come at a heavier price."

Hanuman's eyes followed Rama's gaze to the distant figure of Ravana, his mind turning over the possibilities like pieces on a game board. He had seen Ravana's expressions during the heat of battle—the confidence that masked a deeper fear, the pride that hid cracks in his composure. It was time to use those weaknesses, to turn Ravana's own mind into a battlefield.

"Lord Rama," Hanuman began, his voice low but firm, "strength alone will not break Ravana's hold on his troops. He is driven by pride, by the belief that he is untouchable, that no mortal can challenge his rule. But I have seen the fear in his eyes, the moments when he falters. If we can strike at the core of that fear, we can weaken his resolve and break the spirit of his army."

Rama turned to him, curiosity and hope flickering in his eyes. "What do you propose, Hanuman?"

Hanuman's expression was thoughtful as he gestured towards the battlefield below. "Ravana's greatest strength is the belief his soldiers have in his invincibility, in his command over both the physical and the supernatural. But if we can show them that even Ravana is vulnerable, that his power is not absolute, we will create a crack in their resolve. We must turn his own pride against him, make him feel the pressure of his own image."

He paused, then continued, his voice sharpening with determination. "We must challenge him directly, forcing him to confront his fears—his fear of defeat, his fear of losing control.

And there is one way to do it that he cannot ignore: by using the divine weapons that he believes are beyond our reach."

Rama and Lakshmana exchanged glances, understanding dawning in their eyes. The divine weapons—mystical arrows and celestial powers—were gifts from the gods, artifacts that Ravana himself had sought to hoard as proof of his dominion. To use them against him would not only wound his pride but show his followers that their king's supremacy was not unchallenged.

Rama's voice took on a note of resolve. "You are right, Hanuman. Ravana must see that the gods do not favor him alone, that their power stands with us. But we must choose the moment carefully, when his arrogance blinds him to the danger."

Hanuman nodded, his mind already forming a plan. "There will be a time, during the heat of battle, when Ravana's anger overtakes his judgment. That is when we must strike—using the divine weapons to break through his defenses, to shatter the illusion of his invincibility in front of his own army. It will be like striking at the heart of a storm, disrupting the winds that hold it together."

The next day, as the battle resumed, Hanuman's strategy began to unfold. He directed small units to engage Ravana's forces at different points, using quick strikes to harass and frustrate the demon king's movements. With each skirmish, Ravana's frustration grew, his commands to his troops becoming more erratic, more desperate. It was a subtle shift, but Hanuman could see it in the way the demons hesitated, the way they glanced towards their leader with questions in their eyes.

Then, as the sun reached its zenith, Hanuman signaled to Rama. It was time.

Rama drew one of the divine arrows from his quiver, its tip glowing with the light of the gods, and nocked it against his bow. With a nod to Hanuman, he aimed towards the center of the battlefield, where Ravana's chariot loomed like a dark storm cloud.

The arrow flew, a streak of light against the midday sky, and struck the ground before Ravana's chariot with a thunderous roar. The earth trembled, and a shockwave rippled through the ranks of the demons, their eyes widening as they beheld the power that had been unleashed. But more than the physical force of the attack, it was the meaning behind it that struck at the heart of their confidence—the sight of their king reeling before a power that he had believed he alone could command.

Ravana's expression twisted with rage and disbelief, his ten heads turning as if to defy the very heavens. "You dare to challenge me with the weapons of the gods?" he roared, his voice carrying across the battlefield. But Hanuman could see the flicker of fear beneath the anger, the realization that his enemy's strength was not to be dismissed.

As Ravana unleashed his counterattack, directing a volley of dark magic towards Rama's forces, Hanuman took to the air, leading a charge that struck at the flanks of the demon army. He moved with the precision of a general who knew the terrain of the mind as well as the battlefield, coordinating the movements of his warriors to keep the pressure on Ravana's forces, to drive them back inch by inch.

Each time Ravana tried to regain control, to rally his troops with threats and promises, another divine arrow struck the ground, another display of power that reminded his soldiers that their king was not beyond defeat. Hanuman's plan worked like a slow poison, seeping into the hearts of the demons, eroding their belief in the inevitability of Ravana's rule.

In the final hours of the battle, as the sun dipped low on the horizon and the shadows grew long, Hanuman watched from a hilltop as the tides of war turned decisively. Ravana, his chariot damaged and his once-proud army in disarray, found himself facing Rama directly on the field. But even as the two leaders clashed, Hanuman knew that the outcome had been shaped long before the first blow was struck. It had been shaped in the minds of Ravana's followers, in the seeds of doubt that Hanuman had planted, in the realization that their king could bleed.

As Rama's arrow found its mark, piercing through Ravana's defenses and striking the heart of his power, the demon king's roar of defiance faded into silence. The battlefield fell quiet, and the demons who had once followed Ravana without question now stood uncertain, their eyes turned towards the one who had broken their illusion of invincibility.

Hanuman stood with Rama as the dust settled, the two of them surveying the battlefield where Ravana's banners now lay trampled in the sand. And though the victory had come through strength, Hanuman knew that it was the battle of minds, the calculated strikes against pride and certainty, that had truly decided the day.

Rama turned to Hanuman, a look of deep respect in his eyes. "You have done more than fight at my side, Hanuman. You have shown me the power of seeing beyond the battlefield, of understanding the heart of our enemy. This victory belongs as much to your wisdom as to our arms."

Hanuman bowed his head, a quiet satisfaction filling his heart. "The mind is a battlefield like any other, my lord. And in understanding our enemy's fears, we have won a victory that will be remembered not just for the force of arms but for the insight that guided them."

As the sun dipped below the horizon, casting a red glow over the conquered city, Hanuman knew that the war had ended not just with the fall of a king, but with the breaking of a spell that had held a people in thrall. It was a lesson that would endure beyond the battlefields of Lanka—a lesson in the power of seeing the enemy's mind, of using each word and each strike to shape the future.

And as he stood beside Rama, watching the fires of victory burn in the distance, Hanuman felt the weight of his role as both warrior and tactician—a role that had turned the tide of a war, and perhaps, of history itself.

Chapter 9

THE ROLE OF A DIPLOMAT IN VICTORY AND AFTERMATH

Key Takeaways

- *Bridge the Transition:* Hanuman helps Vibhishana gain trust from Ravana's former followers. Similarly, when Microsoft's Satya Nadella transformed the company culture from Steve Ballmer's aggressive style to a collaborative one, bringing longtime employees on board with the new vision

- *Listen to Opposition:* Giving voice to dissenting demon leaders rather than silencing them. Similar to how successful merger CEOs retain key talent from acquired companies instead of cleaning house, acknowledging their concerns and value

- *Balance Old and New:* Integrating Ravana's former officers into the new system while reforming it. Similar to how digital transformation leaders succeed by balancing legacy systems/employees with new technology/talent, rather than completely starting over

- *Build Trust Gradually.* Moving from conflict to conversation through small victories. Similar to how Netflix transformed from DVD rental to streaming giant - not overnight, but through careful steps that brought customers and stakeholders along

- *Lead Through Service.* Vibhishana showing he'll serve all people, not just supporters. Similar to how successful tech companies pivot from "move fast and break things" to "responsible innovation" - showing they serve society, not just shareholders

The drums of war had fallen silent, replaced by the softer sounds of rebuilding—a hammer striking stone, the murmur of voices seeking to find their new place in a changed world. Lanka, once the proud fortress of the demon king Ravana, now lay beneath a different kind of tension—the uncertainty of a kingdom caught between the past and an unfamiliar future. Ravana was defeated, his rule brought to an end by the hands of Rama and his allies. But the task of healing, of rebuilding a broken kingdom, required a different kind of strength—one that spoke not with weapons but with words, with the power to bridge divides and guide hearts.

As Vibhishana, Ravana's younger brother, took up the mantle of king, Hanuman remained by his side, recognizing that the end of battle did not mean the end of his mission. Vibhishana was a man of integrity, committed to the principles of dharma, but he faced a challenge that even his newfound crown could not shield him from—the distrust and resentment of those who had served Ravana, who saw the new ruler as a betrayer, a puppet of their enemies. Without careful guidance, Hanuman knew, these fractures could undo the hard-won peace, turning a victory into a new kind of conflict.

The new king's first challenge came sooner than expected, in a meeting convened within the great hall of Lanka's palace—a place where the ghosts of past power still lingered in the air. Hanuman sat beside Vibhishana, his eyes calm but watchful as the leaders of Lanka's various factions assembled. The atmosphere was charged, voices rising and falling like waves crashing against a rocky shore. Some spoke with hope for a new beginning, but others, their faces hard with anger, demanded answers, their words edged with bitterness.

"We fought under Ravana's banner," one of the demon leaders said, his voice carrying the heat of old loyalties. "He was our king, and now we are asked to kneel before the brother who stood against him, who brought outsiders to our shores. How are we to trust that this new rule will be any different, any better for our people?"

Murmurs of agreement rippled through the assembly, and Vibhishana's face tightened, a shadow of frustration passing over his features. Hanuman sensed the moment's fragility, how quickly it could spiral into division. But he also saw the opportunity hidden within the dissent—an opening to plant the seeds of unity, to transform doubt into dialogue.

Before Vibhishana could respond, Hanuman rose to his feet, his presence commanding attention. He spoke with a voice that carried both authority and warmth, like a breeze that could soothe even as it swept through the room.

"I understand your fears," he began, his gaze sweeping across the faces of the gathered leaders. "You have lost a ruler, a way of life that you believed in. Change is never easy, especially when it comes at the hands of war. But let us remember what truly lies before us now. The question is not whether to honor the past, but how to build a future that honors all who live in this land."

He paused, letting the weight of his words sink in, then turned to Vibhishana, addressing him directly but speaking so that all could hear. "Vibhishana, you have taken up the throne, but your task is more than to rule. It is to heal the wounds of this kingdom, to show that your commitment to dharma is not just a commitment to the gods, but to the people who stand before you. A ruler who listens, who welcomes even those who once opposed him, is the ruler who truly brings peace."

Vibhishana's expression softened, and he nodded, his voice taking on a new note of humility. "You are right, Hanuman. This kingdom has suffered much, and my duty is to serve all its people, not just those who welcomed my rise. I promise you, I will lead with justice and compassion, and I will hear your grievances. But I ask for your patience, your trust that together, we can build something better than the past we have known."

The demon leader who had spoken earlier eyed Vibhishana warily, but the sharpness in his gaze began to dull, replaced by a flicker of consideration. He glanced at Hanuman, then back to Vibhishana. "We will hold you to that promise, Vibhishana," he said finally, his tone less confrontational. "But know that our patience has limits. Words must become actions."

Hanuman's lips curved into a faint smile, recognizing the shift in the air—a shift from outright hostility to the beginnings of dialogue. It was a small victory, but one that could grow, like the first green shoots emerging from a charred field. As the meeting continued, Hanuman guided the discussion with the deft touch of a diplomat, ensuring that every voice was heard, that grievances were acknowledged without allowing bitterness to take root.

In the days that followed, he remained close to Vibhishana, advising him on the nuances of leadership—how to balance firmness with empathy, how to address the needs of those who had suffered under Ravana's rule without alienating those who had once benefited from it. He helped the new king draft decrees that would restore the rights of the common people, but also measures that would ensure that Ravana's former officers were not cast aside but given a role in the rebuilding.

One evening, as the sun dipped low over Lanka's smoldering ruins, casting long shadows across the palace courtyard, Hanuman and Vibhishana walked among the workers who were beginning to repair the city's walls. Vibhishana's face was drawn with the weight of his new responsibilities, but his steps were steady, his voice carrying a quiet determination.

"I see now why Rama trusted you so deeply, Hanuman," Vibhishana said, his tone thoughtful. "Your strength is not just in the battlefield but in knowing the hearts of others. Without your counsel, I would have faced a kingdom divided, unable to find common ground with those who look upon me with suspicion."

Hanuman inclined his head, but there was a gentle firmness in his reply. "A king's strength lies in his ability to build bridges, not walls. You have within you the power to unite this land, to become a ruler who is remembered not for the battles he won but for the peace he forged. But know that this is a task that requires constant care, like tending a flame that must not be allowed to die."

Vibhishana nodded, understanding the wisdom in Hanuman's words. They stood together in silence for a moment, watching as the workers raised new stones to replace the ones that had fallen, as children played among the scaffolds, their laughter a sound that had been absent for too long. In that moment, Hanuman saw the future that might be possible—a future where the scars of war could heal, where the fires of conflict could give way to the warmth of community.

Yet he also knew that this future would not come easily. It would take time, and it would take the vigilance of those who understood that peace, like war, was a struggle of its own—a struggle to keep hope alive, to transform old hatreds into new understandings.

As the stars emerged above Lanka that night, Hanuman felt a quiet satisfaction settle in his heart. He had played many roles in this story—scout, warrior, strategist—but it was this role, as a guide in the aftermath of battle, that felt most essential. For in these moments, he saw the true fruits of victory—not in the fall of an enemy, but in the rise of something better in its place.

And as he prepared to return to Rama's side, to bring word of Vibhishana's progress and to continue his service to a greater cause, Hanuman knew that the lessons learned here would endure. He had shown that a diplomat's work does not end when the swords are sheathed; it continues in the quiet conversations, in the patient building of trust, in the effort to weave the threads of a fractured world into a new tapestry.

In the shadow of the new dawn over Lanka, Hanuman knew that the battles won with words would last longest of all, shaping a legacy that would outlive even the most storied victories. It was a legacy of peace born from conflict, of understanding forged from struggle—a legacy that, like Hanuman himself, carried the strength to change the world.

Chapter 10

LEGACY OF HANUMAN - WISDOM BEYOND TIME

Key Takeaways

- *Power Needs Wisdom:* Hanuman teaching that power is like the sea - needs control. Like how Apple under Tim Cook balances innovation with responsibility - tech power guided by ethical considerations

- *Create Future Leaders:* Hanuman's legacy living on through others he taught. Similar to how Microsoft's alumni network created dozens of tech leaders and founders - proving great leaders breed more leaders

- *Service Above Status:* Hanuman focusing on duty rather than glory. Think Patagonia's founder giving away his company to fight climate change - showing true leadership serves a greater purpose

- *Balance Force with Restraint*: Hanuman knowing when to use strength vs wisdom. Like how successful CEOs like Satya Nadella succeed through collaborative leadership rather than Steve Jobs-style force of will

- *Build Lasting Impact*: Hanuman's teachings surviving centuries. Similar to how Nelson Mandela's reconciliation approach in South Africa created a template for peaceful transitions that outlived his presidency

The sun cast its final rays across the sea as evening approached, turning the waters into a field of molten gold. In the quiet that settled over the shores of Lanka, Hanuman stood beside Rama, the two figures silhouetted against the horizon. The battles had been fought, the kingdom was on a path to healing under Vibhishana's rule, and the time for farewells had come. Yet, as the waves whispered against the sand, there was a sense that this moment was not merely an ending, but a transition—a turning of the page to a story that would continue beyond their own lives.

Rama's face, lit by the soft glow of the setting sun, held a calm that spoke of a mission fulfilled, but his eyes reflected a deeper thoughtfulness. He turned to Hanuman, who stood beside him with the quiet strength of a mountain that has weathered many storms. The two shared a bond that had been forged in the fires of war, but tempered by the understanding of duty, sacrifice, and the nature of true power.

"Hanuman," Rama began, his voice gentle but resonant with the weight of unspoken questions, "you have been more than an ally in this journey. You have shown me the path through darkness, not just with your strength but with your wisdom. Now that our battles are done, I wish to understand the heart of that wisdom. Tell me, what do you believe is the true nature of power?"

Hanuman considered the question, the sea breeze stirring his fur as he looked out over the water, his mind turning over the lessons he had learned—lessons that had guided him from the jungles of Kishkindha to the burning streets of Lanka. When he spoke, his voice held the cadence of the ancient winds that had carried him across oceans and through the halls of kings.

"Power, my lord, is like this sea," Hanuman said, gesturing to the endless expanse before them. "It can shape the land, carve new paths through rock, and sustain life. But it can also destroy, swallowing everything in its path. True power lies not in force alone, but in understanding when to unleash it and when to hold it back. It is the balance between strength and restraint, between the might of the wave and the patience of the tide."

Rama listened, nodding slowly, but his gaze remained fixed on Hanuman's face, seeking deeper truths. "You speak of balance, Hanuman, but what of duty? What of the weight that we carry, the decisions that change the lives of those who follow us?"

Hanuman's eyes softened, and a small smile touched his lips—one that spoke of a long journey through questions much like these. "Duty, like power, is a burden that can either crush or uplift. It is a fire that can burn the one who bears it, or a light that can guide others through darkness. As leaders, our duty is not only to act but to understand the consequences of our actions—to be a bridge between the needs of the present and the possibilities of the future."

He paused, his expression growing serious as he turned fully to Rama, his voice filled with the sincerity of a lifelong vow. "You have shown me, my lord, that duty means fighting for what is right, even when the path is hard. But it also means knowing when to lay down the sword, to build rather than to destroy. It is a lesson that will remain with me, wherever my path leads."

Rama looked at Hanuman, a deep respect shining in his eyes. He placed a hand on Hanuman's shoulder, a gesture of brotherhood and gratitude. "You have carried this kingdom, this world, on your shoulders, Hanuman. And in doing so, you have shown us all that true greatness lies not in claiming glory, but in the humility to serve others. I have no doubt that your wisdom will live on, guiding those who come after us."

As they stood together, the sun dipped below the horizon, leaving behind a sky painted in hues of violet and gold—a sky that seemed to mirror the fading of an age and the dawn of something new. Hanuman felt a sense of peace settle in his heart, but he also knew that his journey was far from over. The lessons he had learned, the strength he had discovered within himself, were meant to be shared with those who sought to build a world where power served wisdom, not the other way around.

In the days that followed, Hanuman traveled across the lands, his presence becoming a symbol of hope and renewal. He spoke not of conquest but of compassion, not of dominance but of understanding. And wherever he went, he carried the stories of the war, not as a warrior's boast but as teachings—stories of how battles were won not just on the field, but in the hearts of those who dared to believe in a better way.

Lessons for a New Age

The legacy of Hanuman, as time passed, became more than tales of heroism. It became a touchstone for those who sought to lead with integrity, for those who faced challenges that required not only strength but insight. Kings and counselors, soldiers and scholars—each found something in Hanuman's story that resonated with their own struggles, their own search for meaning in the exercise of power.

They learned from his ability to adapt, to see the shape of an enemy's mind and turn it against itself. They saw in his role as a diplomat the power of words to heal, to unite, and to transform even the most entrenched conflicts. And they found in his relationship with Rama a model of loyalty that transcended personal ambition, that placed the welfare of others above the desire for recognition.

In the centuries that followed, as kingdoms rose and fell, as the world changed beyond recognition, Hanuman's legacy endured. His teachings were written into the scriptures, his stories shared around campfires and in royal courts, becoming parables for those who sought guidance in uncertain times. And in every retelling, one theme remained constant: the idea that true leadership is the art of balancing strength with wisdom, of knowing when to wield power and when to temper it with understanding.

A Timeless Dialogue

In a quiet corner of the world, under a sky filled with stars, a young prince once asked his advisor, "What makes a leader great?" And the advisor, with a thoughtful smile, recounted the story of a monkey who crossed oceans, who set cities ablaze not out of anger but to light a path to freedom, and who stood beside a king, not as a subject, but as a friend who understood the weight of duty.

He spoke of the night when Hanuman and Rama stood by the sea, reflecting on the nature of power, and how those reflections had shaped a legacy that outlived both. The young prince listened, and in the words, he found a vision of what he might become—a leader who could guide with the strength of a warrior but also the heart of a sage.

As the story ended, the advisor looked up at the stars and whispered a prayer to Hanuman, the diplomat and the tactician, the guardian of wisdom. He knew that somewhere, beyond the reach of time, the spirit of that ancient hero still walked among the wind and the forests, a reminder that the greatest victories are not those that break the body but those that lift the spirit.

Eternal Relevance

In the end, Hanuman's story is not bound by the time in which it was lived. It speaks to all who seek to understand the complexities of leadership, who struggle with the weight of decisions that shape the lives of others. It is a story that transcends the battlefield, reaching into the chambers where leaders must choose between the easy path and the right one, between the use of force and the power of persuasion.

Hanuman's life teaches that the strength of a leader is not measured by the armies they command but by the hearts they touch, by the willingness to stand between the weak and the strong, to guide with humility as well as with might. His story is a reminder that even in a world that seems divided, there is always a place for those who seek to build bridges, who see beyond the immediate and envision a future where wisdom guides strength.

And so, as the echoes of his story continue to resonate across the ages, Hanuman remains a guide for all who would lead—a guide whose legacy endures in the quiet moments when a leader pauses to consider not just the outcome of their actions, but the impact of their choices on the world they hope to leave behind. It is a legacy that speaks of hope, of resilience, and of the enduring power of a heart that remains unbroken, even in the face of the greatest challenges.

In this way, Hanuman's wisdom remains beyond time—a flame that burns in the heart of those who dare to lead with both strength and compassion, a light that continues to illuminate the path through darkness, guiding those who seek to make their world a better place.

> *"The best leaders aren't remembered for what they conquered,
> but for what they built from the ruins."*
>
> – Dr. Lal Bhatia.

CONCLUSION:
HANUMAN'S ENDURING RELEVANCE

Key Takeaways

- Balance Power with Wisdom: Hanuman's strength guided by strategic restraint. Like how successful tech CEOs (e.g. Jensen Huang of NVIDIA) balance aggressive innovation with responsible AI development - knowing when to accelerate and when to put on the brakes

- *Master Multiple Roles*: Hanuman shifting between warrior, diplomat, and strategist. Similar to Bob Iger's leadership at Disney - moving smoothly between creative visionary, deal-maker, and operational leader depending on what the moment demands

- *Lead Through Understanding.* Hanuman's ability to read situations and hearts. Think Jacinda Ardern's COVID crisis management - combining firm policy with emotional intelligence and clear communication

- *Build Lasting Change.* Hanuman focusing on rebuilding, not just winning. Like Satya Nadella transforming Microsoft's culture from competition to collaboration - showing that changing hearts matters more than changing policies

- *Create Legacy Through Others.* Hanuman's wisdom living on through generations. Similar to how Nelson Mandela's reconciliation approach created a template for peaceful transition that transformed not just South Africa but inspired leaders worldwide

As the last pages of Hanuman's story turn, we find ourselves left not merely with the echoes of battles won and enemies vanquished, but with the enduring presence of a figure whose wisdom extends far beyond the fields of war. Hanuman's journey is one of transformation—from the valiant warrior who leaped across oceans to the diplomat who soothed wounds with words, from the strategist who saw beyond the clamor of battle to the guide who helped rebuild a fractured kingdom. His legacy is not defined by the strength of his arms alone, but by the depth of his insight and the grace with which he wielded his gifts.

At his core, Hanuman embodies a balance that is as rare as it is powerful. His strength was never unchecked, his actions never driven by impulsive fury. Instead, he understood that true power lay in choosing when to unleash his might and when to hold it back. It is this mastery of balance—between action and contemplation, between force and diplomacy—that made him not just a hero of myth but a timeless exemplar of leadership.

In every phase of his journey, Hanuman's strategies went beyond physical conquest. When he crossed the ocean to Lanka, it was not just his leap that made an impact, but the precision with which he gathered intelligence, reading the landscape of enemy territory as one might read a scroll of ancient wisdom. When he stood in Ravana's court, allowing himself to be captured, it was not defeat but a carefully orchestrated play, a maneuver to sow doubt and fear in the hearts of his enemies. And when he set Lanka aflame, it was not an act of rage, but a signal fire—a message to friend and foe alike that the time for change had come.

Yet, even in these moments of strategic brilliance, it was Hanuman's compassion that left the deepest marks. His meeting with Sita in the shadowed garden of Ashoka Vatika was a moment where the battlefield became one of emotions, where hope was the weapon that could pierce through the darkest despair. His ability to see into the hearts of others, to offer solace and encouragement, showed a wisdom that understood the weight of suffering and the power of a single spark of hope.

It is this blend of strength and empathy, of strategic acumen and emotional intelligence, that makes Hanuman's story resonate across time. He was a leader who understood that to win battles was not enough; one must also win hearts, for it is in the hearts of people that true change begins. He knew that diplomacy was not a tool of weakness but of strength—a means to build bridges where others saw only chasms, to find common ground even when the soil seemed barren.

Lessons for a Modern World

As we reflect on Hanuman's legacy, we are reminded that the qualities that made him a legend are not bound to the ancient world. Today's leaders, whether they guide nations, organizations, or movements, face challenges that require the same blend of courage and wisdom, the same ability to see beyond the immediate to the long-term consequences of their choices.

In a world where conflicts are no longer fought with swords and arrows but with ideas, with policies, and with the battle for hearts and minds, Hanuman's approach offers a path forward. He teaches us that foresight is the key to navigating complexity, that understanding one's opponents—and one's allies—is as crucial as any strategic position. He reminds us that strength without compassion is a hollow force, that the greatest victories are those that bring healing, not just triumph.

The story of Hanuman also speaks to the power of adaptability. He moved seamlessly between roles—warrior, diplomat, tactician—understanding that leadership requires the ability to shift perspectives, to approach each challenge with fresh eyes. It is a lesson for all who face a rapidly changing world, where the ability to adapt is often the difference between success and failure.

A Call to Reflection

As we close the book on Hanuman's journey, we are left with a challenge—a call to look beyond the myths and see the enduring relevance of his life. In our own lives, in our communities, and in the arenas where we strive for change, can we learn to balance strength with empathy? Can we be both fierce in our convictions and flexible in our approach? Can we, like Hanuman, recognize that sometimes the most powerful act is not to strike but to listen, to understand, and to build?

Hanuman's legacy is not one that asks us to follow in his footsteps precisely, for his path was uniquely his own. Rather, it invites us to embrace the qualities that made him exceptional: the courage to face overwhelming odds, the wisdom to see through the fog of conflict, and the humility to place others' needs before our own. It is a legacy that endures not in monuments or temples but in the choices we make when faced with adversity—in the moments when we choose to be the bridge, to light the way for others.

In the story of Hanuman, we find the blueprint for a new kind of heroism—one that does not shy away from strength, but that understands its true purpose. It is a heroism that finds power in restraint, victory in understanding, and immortality in the hearts it touches.

May we, like Hanuman, find the strength to leap into the unknown, the wisdom to navigate its challenges, and the grace to leave behind a world that is better for our having been here. For in the end, his story is not just a tale of ancient battles, but a guide for all who seek to lead with vision, with courage, and with a heart that remains unyielding, even in the face of the greatest trials.

And so, as the last light of day fades from the horizon, Hanuman's legacy continues to shine—bright, unwavering, and eternal—a reminder that true power lies not in domination but in the quiet, enduring strength of a soul that knows its purpose.

SELECTED BIBLIOGRAPHY

Ancient Texts and Scriptures

1. **Valmiki, Maharishi.** *Ramayana.* Circa 500 BCE.

   The foundational epic detailing Lord Rama's life, with Hanuman's pivotal role in rescuing Sita, symbolizing devotion and valor.

2. **Vyasa, Sage.** *Mahabharata.* Circa 400 BCE.

   Features Hanuman's encounter with Bhima and his presence on Arjuna's chariot during the Kurukshetra war, exemplifying strength and humility.

3. **Various Authors.** *Puranas.* Circa 300–1500 CE.

   Includes texts like the *Shiva Purana* and *Vishnu Purana*, which provide accounts of Hanuman's divine birth, exploits, and unwavering devotion to Rama.

4. **Tulsidas, Goswami.** *Hanuman Chalisa.* 16th century.

   A 40-verse devotional hymn extolling Hanuman's virtues, recited widely for spiritual strength and protection.

5. **Tulsidas, Goswami.** *Hanuman Bahuk.* 16th century.

   A devotional hymn seeking Hanuman's blessings for healing and overcoming life's challenges.

Modern Analyses and Articles

6. **Vanamali.** *Hanuman: The Devotion and Power of the Monkey God.* Rochester, VT: Inner Traditions, 2010.

   Explores Hanuman's spiritual teachings and their relevance to leadership and personal growth.

7. **Katta, Srini.** *Rama, Lakshmana and Hanuman: Brothers-In-Arms.* Austin, TX: Self-published, 2024.

   A retelling of the Ramayana emphasizing leadership, ethics, and personal growth through the roles of Rama, Lakshmana, and Hanuman.

8. **Jaishankar, S.** *The India Way: Strategies for an Uncertain World.* New Delhi: HarperCollins India, 2020.

   Examines strategic insights from Indian epics, including Hanuman's diplomacy, and applies them to contemporary geopolitics.

9. **Swaroopananda, Swami.** "Valuable Leadership Lessons from Hanuman." *Speaking Tree,* 2015.

   Highlights Hanuman's humility, adaptability, and team leadership qualities.

10. "7 Life-Lessons We Can Learn from Lord Hanuman." *PRATHA,* 2022.

   Outlines lessons on inner strength, resilience, and practical problem-solving inspired by Hanuman.

11. "5 Leadership Lessons from Hindu God, Hanuman." *NYK Daily,* 2020.

    Discusses Hanuman's leadership strategies in communication, confidence, and decision-making.

12. "Management Lessons from Ramayana." *SlideShare,* 2017.

    Analyzes Hanuman's actions in the Ramayana, offering insights into strategic planning and leadership.

13. **Sastry, Manogna, and Subramanian, Arun.** "The Dharma of Leadership Exemplified by Hanuman." *International Journal of Studies in Public Leadership,* 2020.

    Investigates Hanuman's dharmic principles in leadership, diplomacy, and judgment.

14. "HANUMAN: Part I—The Diplomat in Disguise." *Patheos,* 2023.

    Explores Hanuman's diplomatic acumen and its impact on alliances.

15. "Why Bharat Matters in Amrit Kaal: Lessons from Ramayana." *Samvada World,* 2023.

    Applies Hanuman's strategies to modern diplomacy and leadership challenges.

16. "Learning Leadership from Shree Hanuman." *Lunar Astro Vedic Academy,* 2022.

    Examines Hanuman's adaptability and influence, particularly his mastery of 'Mahima.'

17. "How Hanuman Offers Lessons for Public Diplomacy Today." *The Print,* 2023.

Analyzes Hanuman's diplomatic skills and their relevance in contemporary public diplomacy.

18. **Srinivasan, Prime Point.** "Echoes of Humility: Hanuman's Lessons for Modern-Day Leaders." *PreSense,* June 2024.

    Discusses Hanuman's effective communication style and its application in governance and leadership.

19. **Chinmaya Upahar.** "Life and Leadership Lessons from Hanuman." *Chinmaya Upahar Blog,* 2017.

    Highlights Hanuman's qualities of strength, humility, and commitment as leadership lessons.

20. **Modern Wazir.** "Personifying Leadership Qualities of Lord Hanuman for a Successful Corporate Life." *Modern Wazir Blog,* 2023.

    Applies Hanuman's leadership qualities to corporate success.

21. **Sangri Today.** "Hanuman Wisdom: Bridging Ancient Virtues & Modern Leadership." *Sangri Today,* February 2024.

    Explores how Hanuman's virtues can enhance modern leadership practices.

22. **World History Encyclopedia.** "Hanuman." *World History Encyclopedia,* July 2016.

    Provides an overview of Hanuman's role in Indian mythology and the Ramayana.

23. **Learn Religions.** "Lord Hanuman, the Hindu Monkey God." *Learn Religions,* May 2018.

    Discusses Hanuman's significance in Hinduism and his portrayal in the Ramayana.

24. **Vedantu.** "Hindu Scripture: Significance, List of Hindu Scriptures." *Vedantu,* 2023.

    Overview of Hindu scriptures, including texts that feature Hanuman.

25. **Oxford Centre for Hindu Studies.** "Hanuman: The Devotee as Hero." *Journal of Hindu Studies,* 2019.

    Examines Hanuman's role as a devotee and hero in Hindu literature and practice.

26. **Hindu American Foundation.** "5 Things to Know About Hanuman." *Hindu American Foundation Blog,* April 2021.
    Highlights key aspects of Hanuman's character and values.

www.ingramcontent.com/pod-product-compliance
Lightning Source LLC
Chambersburg PA
CBHW020843150726
48196CB00002B/204